Books by Carolyn Haywood

J
3-4
HAYWOOD
HOLIDAY

S 030496

Haywood, Carolyn

Merry Christmas from Eddie

DATE DUE			
DEC 1 8 2017			

Merry Christmas From Eddie

Troll Associates

A TROLL BOOK, published by Troll Associates,
Mahwah, NJ 07430

Published by arrangement with William Morrow and Company,
Inc. For information address William Morrow and Company,
Inc., 105 Madison Avenue, New York, New York 10016.

First Troll Printing, 1987

Printed in the United States of America

10   9   8   7   6   5   4   3   2

ISBN 0-8167-1041-4

To my beloved friend, Beatrice Carson Marks

✳ Contents ✳

* 1 *
Eddie's Christmas Card

It was two weeks before Christmas. The shop windows were filled with Christmas gifts, and inside and outside there were Christmas decorations. Along the main street pine branches and electric lights were looped from lamp post to lamp post. On the sidings down at the railroad station there were carloads of evergreen trees waiting to be unloaded and taken to the stores.

The decorations at Mr. Ward's used-car lot were the cause of great excitement. Eddie was the first to see them and he lost no time in spreading the news.

"You should see what Mr. Ward has done over at his used-car lot," said Eddie that morning when he reached school.

"What's he done?" the children cried.

"He has a fire engine right out in front, right on the corner. And guess who he has sitting at the wheel of the fire engine?"

"Who?" the children asked.

"Santa Claus!" shouted Eddie.

That afternoon, as soon as school was over, the children rushed over to Mr. Ward's used-car lot. Sure enough, there under a big wide banner stretched between two poles stood the fire engine, and at the wheel sat a funny little stuffed body, dressed like Santa Claus. On the banner were the words MERRY CHRISTMAS.

"He's a gnome Santa Claus," said Anna Patricia. "He isn't any bigger than Eddie."

The children climbed up on the fire engine to get better acquainted with Santa Claus. They laughed and shouted.

"He's made of a potato sack stuffed with rags," cried Boodles.

"His beard is made of cotton," shouted George.

"Shake hands, Santa Claus," Eddie said, as he

pumped Santa Claus's limp right arm up and down.

"Handle Santa Claus gently," Mr. Ward called out. "He's a little weak in spots." This made the children laugh.

"He's got an awfully funny hat on," said Anna Patricia. "The tassel sticks up in the air. It ought to hang down."

"Now see here," said Mr. Ward, "you mustn't criticize Santa Claus. You'll hurt his feelings."

"I think he's swell," said Eddie, sitting down on the seat beside Santa Claus.

That night, when Eddie got into his bed, he thought about Santa Claus and the fire engine and suddenly an idea came to him. He would get his father to take a photograph of Eddie sitting on the fire engine beside Santa Claus. And he would use copies of the photograph for his Christmas cards. Eddie went to sleep with a smile on his face, thinking of how surprised the children in school would be when they received his Christmas card and saw him sitting beside Santa Claus on the fire engine.

He decided he wouldn't tell anyone about his Christmas card, but it was hard to keep it a secret. Every once in a while he would say to one of his friends, "Just wait until you see my Christmas card. It's going to be super!"

Eddie could hardly wait to have his photograph taken, but his father was out of town so Eddie had to wait until the following Saturday.

Very early on Friday morning it began to snow. Eddie and his brothers, Rudy and the twins, Frank and Joe, were delighted. "Boy, oh, boy!" cried Frank. "Now we'll have some good sledding!"

"It's snowing so hard you can hardly see as far as the corner," said Joe.

"I sure hope it lasts over Christmas," cried Rudy, "so I can do some skiing with the skis I'm going to get."

By the time the boys started out for school, the snow had covered the street and the sidewalks so that the curbstones had completely disappeared. The boys walked single file on the narrow path that had been made by people walking to the bus stop at the corner. At noon it was still snowing, harder than ever. So much snow had fallen that the children were dismissed from school. They were told to go straight home. The children departed, shouting with joy over the unexpected half holiday.

On Saturday morning when Eddie came downstairs he said, "Dad, are you going to take my picture with Santa Claus today?"

"Yes," replied Mr. Wilson, "this afternoon, right after lunch. We'll probably have to shovel the whole way and sweep the snow off of the fire engine."

"It sure is deep," said Eddie, "but it will be tramped down by this afternoon."

But by afternoon it had begun to snow again. "Can't take any pictures in this," said Mr. Wilson, when he came home. "We'll have to wait until tomorrow."

"Well, we'll have to take 'em tomorrow," said Eddie, "because I'm going to use the pictures for my Christmas cards."

On Sunday morning, when Eddie looked out of the window, he thought it looked like the North Pole. Fences and hedges had completely disappeared and lawns, driveways, and streets were all one even white blanket. Nothing stood above the surface of the snow but the houses, trees, and telephone poles. The first-floor windows in the house across the way seemed to Eddie to be peeping over the snow.

When Eddie went outdoors, he sank into the snow up to his waist and it was so heavy he could hardly move. "Dad!" said Eddie, when he came indoors. "Do you think we can take the picture?"

Mr. Wilson was trying to get the highway department at the Town Hall on the telephone. He wanted to find out whether the snowplow would be up in their area soon. When he hung up the receiver he said, "They have no idea when they can get out here, maybe not until tonight."

"Oh, Dad," Eddie cried, "I have to have my picture taken with Santa Claus today. It's going to be my Christmas card."

"Eddie," said Mr. Wilson, "the fire engine is probably buried in the snow and Santa Claus with it."

"But what will I do about my Christmas card?" said Eddie.

"Couldn't you buy a few?" asked his father.

"They wouldn't be me and Santa Claus," said Eddie.

"That's so," said Mr. Wilson. "But is it important that it should be you and Santa Claus?"

"Oh, it's very important," said Eddie. "Nobody else has thought of it but me. My Christmas card will be different from everybody else's."

"And is it important for your Christmas card to be different from all the others?" said his father.

"Uh-huh," said Eddie, with the grin that always made his father laugh.

"Well, if we can ever get out of here, we'll go over this afternoon and see how things are," said Mr. Wilson. "Meanwhile we'd better get the driveway shoveled out before the plow comes through and throws another ton of snow on top of us. Come on boys!"

Each of the brothers got a shovel, and Mr. Wilson and his four helpers set to work to clear the driveway. The snow was so deep they had to take it off in layers. They worked for twenty-minute shifts and then rested ten minutes all through the morning. They stopped for lunch and Eddie's mother said they all ate like bears. In the afternoon they finished their work and by half past two the driveway was shoveled all the way down to the curb.

"What do we do now?" said Eddie, surveying the thick white mass that filled the street.

Before anyone could answer, the snowplow came around the corner, cutting its way through the snow and piling it into a wall on the sidewalk. Eddie watched the plow as it came nearer and nearer. The men on the plow were waving their arms and shouting. Eddie waved his arms and shouted, too.

"Get back," cried Eddie's father. "Eddie, get back." But Eddie was too interested in watching the plow to hear.

Mr. Wilson rushed up to Eddie and grabbed him by the arm, just as the plow reached their driveway. With a great swish, the snow flew into the open driveway and in a second Eddie and his father had so much snow sticking to them that they looked like a couple of snowmen.

By the time the snow that the plow had thrown into the driveway had been cleared away, it was three o'clock. Rudy and the twins went into the house, took off their things, and fell sound asleep. But not Eddie. He was all ready to have his picture taken. So Mr. Wilson got the car out of the garage and he and Eddie drove over to Mr. Ward's used-car lot. They almost passed it, for all the cars were completely covered with snow. There were only slight bumps to show their tops. The fire engine had disappeared altogether. A little red tassel that seemed to be resting on the surface of the snow was the only thing that showed where the fire engine was.

"What do you suppose that red thing is?" Mr. Wilson asked.

"Why, that's the tassel on Santa Claus's hat!" cried Eddie.

"You can't have your picture taken with Santa Claus today," said Mr. Wilson.

"Well, take the picture anyway," said Eddie.

So Mr. Wilson took the picture.

About three days before Christmas, Eddie began to receive Christmas cards. In the first envelope was a photograph of Anna Patricia sitting beside Santa Claus on the fire engine. On the back of the card it said, "Merry Christmas from Anna Patricia and Santa Claus."

When Eddie looked at George's card, there was George sitting up on the fire engine beside Santa Claus. It said, "Merry Christmas from Santa Claus and George."

When Betsy's card arrived, Eddie read, "Betsy and Star with Santa Claus. Merry Christmas." Santa Claus was sitting between Betsy and Star.

The next day Eddie received a card from Boodles. It said, "Me and Santa Claus driving the fire engine. Merry Christmas! Boodles."

On Christmas Eve all of Eddie's friends received his Christmas card. On the back of each one Eddie had printed his message:

Santa Claus on the fire engine
without me.
Merry Christmas from Eddie

And everyone who received a card from Eddie saw that Eddie was not there, and they wondered where Santa Claus and the fire engine were. And what was that tiny speck sticking up out of the snow?

"That," said Eddie, when they asked him about it, "is the tassel on Santa Claus's hat. He's under it."

When Mr. Kilpatrick, the policeman, saw Eddie he said, "Thank you for your Christmas card, Eddie. I liked it very much."

Eddie said, "I liked it, too. It was different."

"That's what I said to Mrs. Kilpatrick, the very words. I said, 'Now here's Eddie Wilson's card. That's a fine card. Trust Eddie to be different.'"

* 2 *
How Santa Claus Delivered Presents

Every year an enormous Christmas tree was set up in front of the Town Hall. It was strung with hundreds of blue electric lights, and on the very tip-top there was a brilliant white star. The lights were always turned on at five o'clock on Christmas Eve, and nearly everyone who lived in the town, and even people who lived out in the country, gathered in the square and sang Christmas carols.

Right on the edge of the town there was a large children's shelter, and the children always came to the Christmas party. After the carol singing each child received a present.

Eddie's father was in charge of the Town Hall Christmas party this year, and the Wilson boys were thrilled. They all felt like Santa Claus himself. One of the most exciting things was getting the big Christmas tree. Mr. Wilson told the boys that they could go with him to get it, and Eddie could hardly wait for the day to arrive.

"Where do we have to go to get it?" Eddie asked one evening.

"Over to the railroad freight station about two miles from here," said Mr. Wilson. "It will be tagged for Town Hall. It's always cut especially for the purpose. In fact, it's always one of the largest trees in the whole country."

"You mean in the whole United States?" asked Eddie.

"That's right," his father replied.

"Where do they cut such a big Christmas tree?" said Eddie.

"Up in Maine," replied Mr. Wilson. "They have to send it down on a railroad car that handles telephone poles."

"How do they put up such a big tree in the square?" Eddie asked.

"Oh, the men who put up the telephone poles put it up," Mr. Wilson answered. "They take a truck over to the station to get the tree."

"Oh, Dad!" Eddie cried. "I thought we were going for the tree."

"We are," said Mr. Wilson. "We are going over in our car, but they are going to do the hauling. Then we'll drive over to the square and watch them put it up. Volunteers from the electric company will string up the lights."

"Won't we do anything but watch 'em?" Eddie asked, looking downcast.

"I think you will find plenty to do," said his father. "You usually do."

For weeks now, the boys and girls in school had been busy repairing and painting toys they had brought to school. These were to be given out at the Christmas party to the children from the children's shelter and children in the hospital. The boys put new wheels on toy wagons and gave them fresh coats of paint so that they looked brand new. The girls made new dresses for the dolls that were brought to school and painted their faces and tied new ribbons on their hair. When they were all finished, the window sills in every classroom were piled high with toys. No one would have been surprised to find Santa Claus himself walking up and down the halls of the school.

"How are we going to get all these toys over to the town square?" Eddie asked one day.

"Mr. Ward has offered to take them over in the old fire engine he keeps on his car lot," said Mrs. Aprili, Eddie's teacher.

"I wonder if he'll let Santa Claus drive them over," said Boodles, laughing.

"The fire engine and Santa Claus were buried in the snow the last time I passed Mr. Ward's," said Eddie. "All you could see was the tassel on Santa Claus's hat."

"Well, Mr. Ward is in charge of the presents," said Mrs. Aprili. "We don't have to worry about them. Mr. Ward said he would get them to the Christmas party and distribute them. I am sure he'll find a way to do it even if his fire engine is buried in the snow."

That day after school Eddie walked over to Mr. Ward's used-car lot. He found Mr. Ward digging the fire engine out of the snow. "Have you got another shovel, Mr. Ward?" Eddie asked. "If you have, I'll help you."

"I certainly have, Eddie," said Mr. Ward, "and I'd be mighty glad of a little help."

"Okay," said Eddie, and when Mr. Ward got the shovel, he set to work.

"I hear you're going to take the toys over to the square on Christmas Eve," said Eddie.

"That's right," Mr. Ward replied. "That's why I have to dig this out of the snow."

"Are you going to take Santa Claus?" asked Eddie.

"Oh, sure!" replied Mr. Ward. "Santa Claus has to go to the big Christmas doings. Santa Claus has to give out the presents."

"But he can't," said Eddie, " 'cause he's only stuffed."

"Well, I've got an idea," said Mr. Ward.

"What is it?" Eddie asked.

Mr. Ward leaned on his shovel while he told Eddie his idea, and Eddie stopped shoveling to listen. Eddie's eyes grew larger and his smile grew broader as Mr. Ward's idea unfolded.

Finally Mr. Ward said, "What do you think of that, Eddie?"

Eddie replied, "I think it's great! I can hardly wait!"

"Well, now, don't tell anyone," said Mr. Ward.

"Not even my father?" said Eddie.

"Oh, I've already talked to your father about it. He thinks it's a good idea."

"Wow! I can hardly wait," said Eddie, as he dug his shovel into the snow.

Finally the day arrived for the big Christmas tree to be put up in the square. Mr. Wilson left his office early and reached home about the same time as Eddie and his brothers. They had come straight home from school because they didn't want their father to go for the tree without them. The four boys climbed into the car and Mr. Wilson started for the railroad station where the Christmas tree was waiting.

"Do you think we'll get there before the men from the telephone company, Dad?" said Eddie. "You don't think they'll get there first and take it away before we get there, do you?"

"They may get there first," said Mr. Wilson, "but they can't take the tree until I get there because I have to sign the receipt for it. It was shipped in my name."

"That's good," said Eddie. "I want to see them put the Christmas tree on the truck."

Just then Mr. Wilson drove around a bend in the road and there, ahead of them, was the telephone truck. It was parked at the side of the road, and the men had their heads under the hood.

Mr. Wilson drove up behind them and stopped his car. He got out and walked to the truck. Eddie and his brothers got out and followed him.

"Hello there!" said Mr. Wilson. "What's the trouble?"

"Oh, hello, Mr. Wilson," said one of the men. "Got some trouble with the truck. Seems to be in the motor."

"She's as dead as a doorknob," said another man. "They'll have to tow her in."

"How will we get the Christmas tree?" asked Rudy.

"We can call up Mr. Ward," said Eddie. "He'll bring the fire engine over."

"Now, Eddie, this is one time we are not going to get the fire engine out," said his father. "Mr. Ward's fire engine isn't long enough to take the tree."

"Tell you what, Mr. Wilson," said one of the men who the other two called Pete, "suppose you drive me back to town. I'll pick up the tow truck and come back for this truck, and maybe I can think of a way to get the tree hauled over."

"Fine," said Mr. Wilson, "we'll start right back."

Meanwhile, Eddie kept saying, "Dad, I think

18

Mr. Ward's fire engine *is* big enough. Why don't you call him?"

Finally Mr. Wilson said, "Now, Eddie, I know it wouldn't be big enough, so forget it. You're not going to ride on the fire engine today."

As Mr. Wilson and Pete walked toward the Wilsons's car, the other two men said, "We'll wait here."

"Okay!" said Pete. "We won't be more than a half hour. You'd better put some flares in the road so you don't get hit."

"We'll build a bonfire, too, so we won't freeze before you get back," said one of the men.

When Rudy and the twins heard there was to be a bonfire they decided to stay with the truck, but Eddie climbed back into his father's car.

"Can I ride back on the tow truck?" he said to Pete as soon as Mr. Wilson had turned the car around.

"Sure!" said Pete.

Mr. Wilson hadn't quite reached the edge of the town when Pete said, "You know what? I'll bet the guys at the firehouse would go over for that tree with the hook-and-ladder truck."

"That's an idea!" said Mr. Wilson. "Maybe they would. Let's stop and ask them."

"Oh, boy!" cried Eddie. "This is going to be great!"

Mr. Wilson drove up to the firehouse where the hook and ladder was kept, and he and Pete and Eddie went in. Mr. Wilson and Pete knew all the firemen, and when Mr. Wilson told them what he wanted, they said, "It's okay with us, but you'll have to ask the chief. He's gone home to dinner."

In a few minutes Mr. Wilson had the chief on the telephone.

"It's okay with me," said the chief. "But you'll have to ask the mayor." So Mr. Wilson telephoned to the mayor, and when the mayor heard the story he said, "Sure! Tell them to take the hook and ladder over. We have to get the tree."

It was no time at all before the firemen, in their heavy coats, were ready to drive the big, shiny red hook and ladder out of the firehouse. Eddie was so excited he was hopping up and down.

"Do you want to come along?" one of the firemen called to him.

"Oh, yes!" cried Eddie.

"Are you bundled up good and warm?" the fireman asked.

"Sure!" said Eddie, as one of the men lifted him up beside the driver.

"Better put these earmuffs on," said one of the men, and he put an enormous pair of earmuffs over Eddie's ears.

Eddie looked as though his face was being held between the paws of a great big bear, with a grin stretching from one paw to the other.

"This is great!" cried Eddie, as he waved good-bye to his father and Pete.

"I'll meet you over at the station," Mr. Wilson called. "I'll drop Pete off for his truck."

Rudy, the twins, and the two telephone men were warming themselves by the fire when they heard the rumbling of a heavy truck approaching.

"Guess this is them," said Rudy.

"Sounds too heavy," said one of the men, looking at the oncoming headlights.

"I'll be hanged if it isn't the hook and ladder!" said the other man, as the firemen drew up behind the telephone-company truck.

"Hi!" cried Eddie to his brothers.

"Look at Eddie!" cried Frank.

"Hey! How did you get up there?" cried Rudy.

"Are you going to get the Christmas tree?" Joe asked.

"You bet we are!" the driver called. "When you want to get something done in these parts, you

have to get the fire department to do it." Everyone laughed.

"Can we come, too?" Frank asked.

"Sure! Everybody up," the driver of the hook and ladder called out.

Eddie's brothers scrambled up, and the hook and ladder started off again. The telephone men shouted "So long!" and waved.

The firemen and the boys waved back. "We'll send a horse and sleigh to tow you in," one of the firemen shouted and everyone laughed.

It was not long before the firemen pulled up alongside the freight station. They all jumped down.

"Where's this Christmas tree we have to haul over to the Town Hall?" the driver asked the man in charge of the freight station.

"Right over on the siding," said the man. "I'll show you."

By the time the firemen had the tree fastened on the hook and ladder, Mr. Wilson had arrived. He signed the receipt for the tree, while the boys climbed back up with the firemen.

"Anybody driving back to town with me?" Mr. Wilson asked.

No one made any reply. "Guess not!" said Mr. Wilson.

"You'll have to get yourself a fire engine, Mr. Wilson, if you want somebody to ride with you," said the stationmaster.

"Looks that way," said Mr. Wilson.

When the firemen and the Wilson boys arrived in front of the Town Hall with the Christmas tree, the telephone men were waiting to put it up. In a very short time they had the big tree in place. As the hook and ladder drove away, the men from the electric company arrived with yards and yards and yards of electric cord and hundreds of blue bulbs.

It was nine o'clock before the job was finished, and then Mr. Wilson suddenly remembered that he and the boys had forgotten all about dinner. He ran to the nearest telephone and called up Mrs. Wilson. When he heard her voice he said, "I'm terribly sorry, but I forgot all about dinner. We've been so busy with the Christmas tree."

"I thought you would," said Mrs. Wilson, "so I baked beans. They're in the oven and it doesn't make any difference if they stay there until next week."

"Baked beans!" cried Mr. Wilson. "I hope you

baked a bushel. Have you got enough for twelve hungry men, including Eddie?"

"I believe so," said Mrs. Wilson, laughing. "Bring them over."

Mr. Wilson went outside and called, "Hey, there are baked beans at our house. Come along, everybody!"

The following evening, about five o'clock, the square in front of the Town Hall was thronged with people. Every face was turned toward the huge Christmas tree. From the belfry of a nearby church came the sound of chimes playing "O Little Town of Bethlehem." As the hands of the Town Hall clock pointed to five o'clock, the lights on the Christmas tree were turned on. The blue lights seemed suddenly to turn the square into a fairyland.

For fifteen minutes the chimes played and all the people in the square sang Christmas carols. When the singing was over, Mr. Wilson spoke from the steps of the Town Hall. He said, "Santa Claus is now driving into the square with his fire engine full of presents for some of our very good boys and girls."

Betsy, who was standing with her mother and

her sister, Star, looked where Mr. Wilson was pointing and saw Mr. Ward driving his fire engine very slowly up to the entrance of the Town Hall. On the seat beside Mr. Ward, leaning against him, was the funny little Santa Claus Mr. Ward had made. When Mr. Ward stood up, Santa Claus toppled right over in a heap and everyone laughed. Then Mr. Ward picked up Santa Claus and handed him down to Mr. Wilson who tucked him under his arm and carried him up the steps of the Town Hall. There he deposited him on the wide brick wall and propped him up against a post. Santa Claus doubled up like a jackknife.

"Now see here, Santa Claus," said Mr. Wilson, "this is Christmas Eve and you have work to do. You'll have to come to life. Just look at all these boys and girls waiting for you to give them their presents." And Mr. Wilson shook Santa Claus very hard.

The children gathered in front of the steps shouted with laughter, but their laughter was soon stopped by their surprise. Very slowly Santa Claus began to straighten up. He stretched one arm out and then the other. Then he began to get up, and suddenly there was a lively little Santa Claus standing on his feet and calling out, "Merry

Christmas! Merry Christmas! Step right up, boys and girls, and get your presents!"

"Why," shouted Betsy, "it's Eddie Wilson inside the Santa! It's Eddie Wilson!"

* 3 *
Christmas Is Coming

One morning in December Eddie pulled a piece of paper out of his pocket. It was his list of celebrations. "Look," he said to Boodles, "we haven't done much celebrating, and this year is almost over. The trouble is nobody likes to celebrate as much as I do."

"We're going to have a big one soon," said Boodles. "The biggest one of the whole year—Christmas—and I haven't bought my mother a Christmas present yet."

"I just have to get one more present," said Eddie. "There's a little kid who just moved in across the street from us. He fell out of bed the other night and broke his arm. I'm going to buy him a toy horse and wagon, 'cause he's crazy about horses. His name is Georgie."

Boodles looked at the list of celebrations that Eddie was holding in his hand. "That's good, Eddie!" he said. "If you buy the little kid a toy, you'll be celebrating 'Be Kind to Somebody Week'! Then you can cross that one off your list."

Eddie laughed. "It'll be a two-in-one celebration."

"I'm going to buy my mother a bird," said Boodles.

"What kind of bird?" Eddie asked.

"She says either a parakeet or a canary," Boodles replied. "But I haven't saved up enough money yet."

"It's getting pretty close to Christmas," said Eddie.

"I know," said Boodles. "Soon as I get the money, will you go with me to get the bird?"

"Sure," Eddie replied. "I'd like to."

The days went by very quickly, and before long it was the day before Christmas. School had closed for the holidays. Suddenly, in the middle of the afternoon, Eddie remembered that he had not bought the horse and wagon for little Georgie. While he was counting the money that he had saved, the telephone rang. Eddie ran to it and picked up the receiver. It was Boodles.

"Say, Eddie!" Boodles shouted into the telephone. "You promised to go with me to buy the bird for my mother's Christmas present. It's almost Christmas Eve!"

"Have you got the money?" Eddie asked.

"Oh, yes!" Boodles replied. "My father gave me some. How about if we go now?"

"Okay!" said Eddie. "I still have to buy Georgie's toy horse and wagon. I'll ask my mother."

In a few minutes Eddie was back on the telephone. "'Hey, Bood," he said, "my dad just came in. He says he has to go get some Christmas lights, so we can go with him. We'll pick you up in fifteen minutes."

"That's great!" said Boodles.

About four o'clock Eddie and his father stopped at Boodles's house. Boodles came out and jumped into the car. As Mr. Wilson drove, he said to the boys, "Now I'll let you out at the pet shop, where Boodles can get his bird. Then you can walk down the street to the department store, where Eddie can get the toy for Georgie. When you come out of the store, wait for me on the curb. I'll pick you up there."

"Okay, Dad!" said Eddie.

Mr. Wilson drove up in front of the pet shop, and the boys got out of the car. "See you later!" said Mr. Wilson, and he drove off.

Eddie and Boodles went into the store. There were a lot of people and a lot of noise from children and puppies. Everyone seemed to be busy selecting puppies or kittens. Eddie and Boodles made their way to the back of the store, where the birdcages were lined up. The boys looked them over.

"I don't know whether to get a parakeet or a canary," said Boodles.

"You have to make up your mind quickly," said Eddie, " 'cause it's almost Christmas Eve and the stores will close soon."

A salesman came up to the boys and said, "Are you interested in a bird?"

"Yes!" Boodles replied. "It's for my mother for Christmas."

"Do you want a parakeet or a canary?" the man asked.

"Which is better?" Boodles asked.

"They're both nice birds," the man replied, "but

they're different. Parakeets talk and canaries sing. It just depends whether you want a talker or a singer."

"Let me hear one talk," said Boodles.

"Oh, you have to teach them to talk," said the man.

"Well then I guess I'd better hear a canary sing," said Boodles.

"My dear boy," said the salesman, "these are not mechanical birds. You have to wait until the bird wants to sing."

"But what if it never wanted to sing?" asked Boodles, looking at the canary in a cage that the man was holding. "Couldn't you make it sing a little bit?"

"No, I can't," said the man, "but I'm sure this canary will sing when it gets into your home. It will be happy, and then it will sing."

"Well, okay!" said Boodles. "I'll take the canary." He put his hand into his pocket and said, "I hope I have enough money." Boodles counted out his money. "Is that enough?"

"You'll need another dollar," said the man.

"I haven't got another dollar," Boodles replied.

"Well, the canary and the cage cost a dollar more than you have here," said the salesman.

Boodles's face fell. He let out a big sigh. "It's almost Christmas Eve," he said, "and I have to find a bird for my mother." He looked at Eddie. "What am I going to do?"

"Here," said Eddie, fishing into his pocket, "I've got two dollars and fifty cents for the horse and wagon. You take a dollar of it, and I'll see what I can buy for Georgie for a dollar and a half."

"Oh, thanks, Eddie! That's super," said Boodles, cheering up. "I'll pay you back."

"I'll put a cover over the cage," said the salesman, as he took Eddie's dollar bill.

Soon the man was back with the cage. He had covered it with a cloth. "Here's your bird," he said. "Take good care of it. Carry it carefully."

"I'll be careful," said Boodles, as he took the cage.

When the boys left the pet shop, they started to walk down the street to the big department store. Boodles was carrying the cage as carefully as he would have carried an egg on a spoon.

"Look, Boodles!" Eddie complained. "If you're going to poke along like that, the department store will be closed before we get there."

"I don't want to jiggle the canary," said Boodles.

"Well, I'll have to hurry," said Eddie, "or I

won't be able to buy the horse and wagon for Georgie."

"Okay, go on!" said Boodles. "I'll find you upstairs on the toy floor."

Eddie set off at a run. In a few minutes he reached the store. As he went in through the revolving door a man standing inside stopped him. "Merry Christmas, son!" he said to Eddie, laying his hand on Eddie's shoulder. The man was wearing a uniform, and Eddie thought he was a policeman.

"Merry Christmas!" Eddie replied, trying to escape the man's grasp.

"Son!" said the man. "You have just won a prize!"

"A prize!" said Eddie. "What for?"

"The store is giving a prize to the ten thousandth child to come through that door," the man replied. "You are the one!"

Eddie's mouth fell wide open in surprise. When he closed it, he said, "What's the prize?"

"You will have to go to the toy department," the man replied, handing Eddie a Christmas wreath. There was a ribbon tied across it. In large letters it said: *The Winner!* "Just take this wreath to Santa," the man said. "He will give you the prize."

Eddie took the wreath and said, "Thanks!" He thought he must be dreaming. Hundreds of other people who were doing their last-minute shopping were rushing into the store. But he was the winner. He felt like a jockey who had won a horse race! As Eddie walked to the escalator, he saw people smiling at him. They stood and watched him as the escalator carried him up to the second floor. Some called out: "Congratulations!" "Good for you!" "Lucky boy!" Eddie began to feel his face turning red.

His face turned redder when he found that he had to stand in a line of little children who were waiting to speak to Santa Claus. Eddie looked them over. There wasn't a child over four years old on the line. He felt like a giant and wished he hadn't won the prize. Then he thought of Boodles crawling along with the canary. He hoped the store would be closed before Boodles arrived. Why hadn't he told Boodles to wait for him outside?

The line was moving slowly. *Why do these little kids have to say so much to Santa Claus?* Eddie said to himself. *By this time, almost Christmas Eve, Santa Claus must be sick of listening to them.* Eddie looked at Santa

Claus. *There he sits!* he thought. *Big as all outdoors! Taking these babies on his knee. Giving out "ho, ho, ho!"* Then, to Eddie's horror, he saw Boodles. Boodles was looking all around for him. Eddie wished he could fall through the floor. He looked the other way, but Boodles spotted him.

"Eddie," Boodles shouted, "for cryin' out loud! Are you waiting to sit on Santa Claus's knee?" Boodles began to laugh. He laughed so hard that he doubled over and had to put the birdcage on the floor.

"Keep quiet!" said Eddie. "I've won a prize."

"What for?" said Boodles, sobering up.

"For coming through the front door at the right time," Eddie answered, holding up the wreath.

"Wow!" said Boodles. "What are you going to get?"

"I don't know," Eddie replied.

"Look, Eddie," said Boodles, "why don't you hold that wreath above your head? Maybe Jolly Old Saint Nick up there will see it and call you up to him."

"Don't know why I didn't think of it," said Eddie, lifting the wreath high above his head. Boodles's suggestion worked. Santa Claus called out, "Why, here's the winner! Come right up!"

Eddie was glad to leave the little children and walk up to Santa Claus. Santa Claus shook Eddie's hand and said, "My congratulations! I hope you'll like your prize. I'm happy to give you this beautiful, big rocking horse!"

Eddie as well as Boodles, who had come with him, looked at the rocking horse. It was indeed a fine rocking horse, but when Santa Claus asked Eddie to get on it, Eddie's ears turned bright red. "Get on! Get on, son!" said Santa Claus. "See what a fine rocking horse it is!"

Eddie threw his leg over the horse, but his feet wouldn't clear the floor. Santa Claus began to rock the horse, so Eddie had to lift his feet and hold them straight out.

Boodles was trying not to laugh, but he couldn't help himself. He ran behind a pillar and leaned against it, rocking with laughter. When he had laughed himself into hiccups, he came back to Eddie, who was waiting for him. "What are you going to do with this rocking horse?" Boodles asked.

"I'm going to give it to little Georgie," Eddie replied. "I'm saving a dollar and a half, and I bet this will be Georgie's favorite Christmas present."

"That's a great idea!" said Boodles. "Is the store going to deliver it for you?"

"No, it's too late," Eddie replied. "I have to take it."

"Do you think you can carry it?" Boodles asked. "It's awfully big."

"Oh, sure!" said Eddie.

"Do you want it wrapped?" one of the sales-clerks asked.

"No thanks!" Eddie replied. "I can carry it better if it isn't wrapped up."

Eddie still had the wreath, so he hung it around the horse's neck. Then he picked up the horse. First he tried to carry it by the head and the tail, but the rockers stuck out in front of him.

"You can't carry it that way!" said Boodles. "You'll poke those rockers into everybody."

Eddie set the rocking horse down and looked at it. He decided that the best way to carry it would be to put his arms around the belly of the horse. When he had it securely in his grasp, the salesclerk said, "Are you sure you can manage it?"

"Of course!" said Eddie, as he started off with Boodles. The horse's head was across Eddie's shoulder, and the wreath hung down from the horse's neck. The rockers knocked against Eddie's legs.

"You'll never get that thing down the escalator," said Boodles.

"I can't see where I'm going," said Eddie, "but if you get me to the escalator, I'll be okay."

Boodles, with the birdcage in one hand, guided Eddie with the other. When they reached the top of the escalator, Boodles said, "It's right here, Eddie. Now get on with your right foot. No, I guess you better get on with your left foot."

"What difference does it make!" Eddie cried. "Just tell me where to put my foot. I can't see!"

"Wait until I put the birdcage down," said Boodles. "Then I'll put your foot on the top step."

Meanwhile, last-minute shoppers were lining up to get on the escalator. "Hurry up!" they shouted. "Get that thing out of the way!" "You'll break your neck if you try to go down with it!"

Suddenly a loud gong rang through the store. It was the closing bell. Now the people behind Eddie shouted more loudly. "Get out of the way! Do you want us to spend the night here? It's Christmas Eve! We'll be locked in!"

Then a young man stepped up to the boys, and

said to Eddie, "Look, kid! Let me have that thing. We'll take the elevator."

"I'll meet you down by the front door," said Boodles as he picked up his birdcage. "I'll go down the escalator."

Eddie followed the young man to the elevator. When they reached the ground floor, he gave the rocking horse back to Eddie. "I have to go the other way," he said. "Have a merry Christmas!"

"Thanks a lot!" said Eddie. "Merry Christmas to you."

Boodles was waiting by the front door when Eddie came along with the rocking horse. People were hurrying to leave. The revolving door went round and round, carrying them from the warmth inside to the cold outside, where it had begun to snow.

"Come on!" said Eddie to Boodles. "I can't see very well, so you have to come in with me."

"Okay!" said Boodles, as he pushed Eddie into one of the sections of the door. "Move in close, Eddie. I can't get the birdcage in."

People were trying to push from behind, so Boodles held the birdcage on top of his head. The door began to move, and when the section that contained Boodles and the birdcage and Eddie and the rocking horse reached the street side, Boodles stepped out. Before Eddie could move, however, someone pushed from behind and Eddie and the rocking horse had to go back into the store. There stood the man who had given the winner's wreath to Eddie. "Sorry folks," he said, "but I'm locking this door now. Kindly use the side exit."

Eddie had to go off with the rocking horse, followed by a crowd of shoppers. By the time he rounded the corner it was snowing hard. The pavements and streets were white. When Eddie reached Boodles, he said, "Have you seen my dad?"

"I've been busy looking for you, so I haven't been able to look for him," Boodles replied.

The boys pushed through the people to the curb. There was a man selling fresh roasted peanuts. Boodles moved close to the stand. He could feel a little warmth. "I hope this canary doesn't catch cold," said Boodles. "I don't want it to sneeze when I give it to my mother."

"I don't see my dad's car," said Eddie, "but maybe he drove around the block."

"I hope this bird's a singer," said Boodles. Just then there was a sound that Boodles was sure came from inside the cage. "Eddie!" Boodles cried. "Did you hear that? Did you? This bird's whistling! Do you hear it?"

"That's the peanut roaster, stupid!" said Eddie, as a horn tooted. "There's my dad!"

Eddie and Boodles made their way to the car. When Mr. Wilson saw the rocking horse in Eddie's arms, he got out of the car. "What have you got there?" he said in surprise.

"It's a rocking horse for little Georgie," said Eddie. "I won it!"

"Good grief!" said his father, as he loaded it into the back of the car. "Some toy horse and wagon!"

The boys climbed into the front of the car. Boodles held the birdcage on his lap. "Gee!" said Boodles. "I sure thought I had a whistler for a minute. I hope I've got a singer."

"Oh, sure you have!" said Eddie.

Boodles put his ear to the top of the cage. "It's awfully quiet," he said. "You don't think it's dead, do you, Eddie?"

"Course not!" Eddie replied.

"I hope it didn't catch cold while we were standing in the snow," said Boodles.

"Oh, stop worrying, Bood!" said Eddie. "You're driving me nuts!"

"It just made a very funny noise," said Boodles.

"Well then it's alive," said Eddie.

"I think it sneezed," said Boodles. "Maybe it's got the flu!"

"It's probably just hungry," said Eddie.

When they reached Boodles's house, Boodles got out of the car. Mr. Wilson handed the cage to him. "Thanks, Mr. Wilson!" said Boodles. "Have a merry Christmas!"

Eddie called out, "If you hear that canary whistle again, you'll know it isn't the peanut roaster. Merry Christmas, Boodles! Merry Christmas."

"Merry Christmas, Eddie!" Boodles replied. "Thanks for being kind to somebody."

When Eddie looked puzzled, Boodles said, "Me! You know! That dollar you loaned me, so that I could buy the bird."

Eddie laughed, and said, "Oh, that! Just a celebration."

* 4 *
How the Christmas Tree Fell Over

As long as Eddie Wilson could remember he and his brothers had left cookies for Santa Claus on Christmas Eve, and Santa Claus had always left a note thanking them for the cookies.

Eddie had asked his friend, Anna Patricia, if she left cookies for Santa Claus and did Santa leave a note. Anna Patricia said, "No." She had never found a note from Santa Claus on Christmas morning.

"Did you leave cookies for him?" Eddie asked.

"Not just for Santa Claus," said Anna Patricia. "But there are always cookies on the table."

"Oh, they have to be especially for him," said Eddie. "Not just a help-yourself plate!"

"Oh," said Anna Patricia, "I guess that's why he never left a note."

Eddie asked other friends, Boodles and Betsy and Billy, if they left cookies for Santa Claus and if Santa Claus left a note thanking them.

"Sounds to me as though Santa Claus is a free-loader," said Boodles.

Eddie said, "Well, he likes to nibble on good cookies."

Eddie began to think it was strange that Santa Claus only left notes at the Wilson house. It puzzled him so much that by the time he was six, he had a suspicion that his father had something to do with Santa Claus. Could it be that his father had been playing Santa Claus and that he had placed the six presents under the tree and left the note?

The year Eddie was seven he had one of his bright ideas. He would have fun fooling his father and his brothers. He would be a second Santa Claus and when everyone came down to breakfast Christmas morning there would be twelve presents under the tree and two notes from Santa Claus.

Eddie's first problem was the six presents. It took

quite some time for Eddie to save up enough money to buy the presents.

For weeks Eddie had thought of nothing but his Christmas surprise. *This will be a great joke on Dad and the boys,* he said over and over to himself. *They must know that Dad has always played Santa Claus, but they didn't tell me.*

By the week before Christmas Eddie had everything settled with a necktie for each of the boys and one for his father. He had a small bottle of perfume for his mother.

On Christmas Eve the family spent the evening as they always had, trimming the Christmas tree. It was always hung with blue lights. As always a night-light was left burning in the living room when they went up to bed.

Eddie went upstairs with the rest of the family. He kissed his mother good-night and got into bed. Then he waited until he heard his father creeping down the stairs.

"Now," said Eddie, "he's going to put the presents under the tree and leave the note that he has written from Santa Claus. He'll put it right beside the cookie plate where he has always placed it."

Eddie was so excited he lay awake listening to his heart beating. It was a long time before Eddie heard the clock strike two. "I guess it's safe to go down now," he said to himself. He picked up his gifts and his note signed "Santa Claus" and made his way to the head of the stairs as quietly as he could, but on the third step he tripped and fell. He caught himself and broke his fall. His gaily wrapped presents were thrown all over the steps. Eddie sat down and held his breath. He hoped no one had heard him for it was no time to wake up the family and spoil everything. He waited, listening for a few minutes. When everything seemed quiet Eddie went downstairs picking up the presents as he went.

When he reached the living room the night-light showed the other six presents under the tree. As Eddie placed his parcels beside them he laughed to himself, thinking of everyone's surprise when they found so many presents from Santa Claus.

Eddie placed his note from Santa Claus beside the one that his father had left.

Feeling very pleased with himself he started to leave the room but he tripped on the cord that connected the Christmas tree to a plug in the wall. Eddie fell and the Christmas tree fell on Eddie. He found himself covered with spruce-tree branches and electric-light bulbs. Eddie lay still and in a few moments he heard his father, in a voice that sounded as though his father was trying to whisper, say, "Is that you, Santa Claus?"

In the same kind of voice, Eddie called back, "Yes."

"Is anything the matter?" his father said.

"I knocked over the Christmas tree," Eddie replied.

In a few moments his father came into the living room. "Why, Santa Claus," he said, "you seem to be in trouble."

Mr. Wilson picked up the Christmas tree and helped Eddie to his feet. He looked at his youngest son and said, "It's strange, Santa Claus, how much you resemble my son, Eddie."

Eddie laughed and threw his arms around his father. "Oh, Dad," he said, "I hope you don't mind."

"I don't mind," said his father. "I think it's a wonderful joke. Do you mind now that you know I've been playing Santa Claus? Does it make you sad?"

"No, it doesn't make me sad," said Eddie, "but I won't tell any of the little kids in the neighborhood. They just love everything about Santa Claus. They feel that he's real, and I'll help to keep

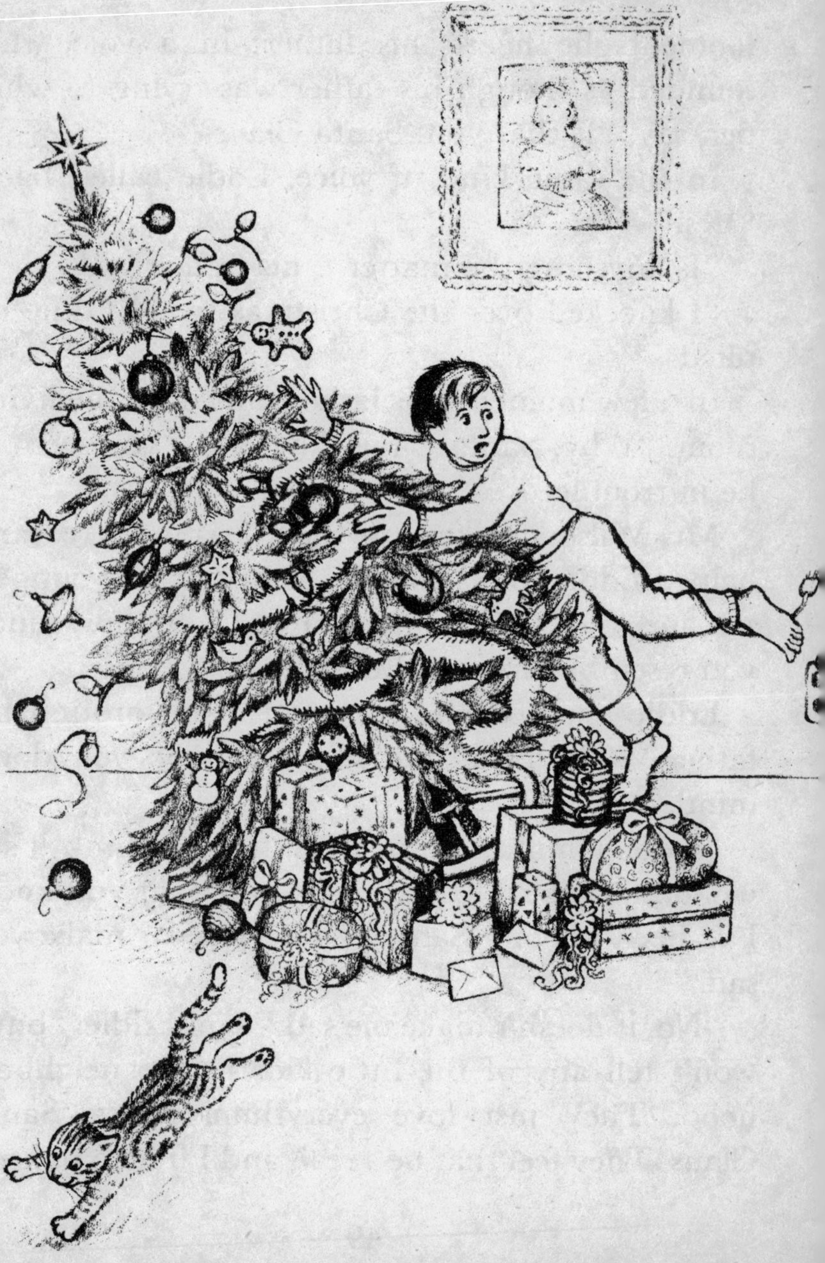

it that way. But, oh, Dad, I have enjoyed being Santa Claus this year."

When his brothers came downstairs and learned what Eddie had done they laughed, and Joe said, "It's just like Eddie."

* 5 *
Christmas Bells for Eddie

Shortly before Thanksgiving Eddie's school learned that their orchestra had been asked to do the Christmas television program. Eddie thought it was wonderful, but he felt sad because he was not in the orchestra. He didn't play any instrument. Sidney, who lived next door, played the cello; Anna Patricia played the clarinet; and Eddie's twin brothers played saxophones.

One morning at breakfast Eddie was bemoaning the fact that he couldn't be in the orchestra. "Mom," he said, "why didn't you make me learn to play something? Then I could be in the orchestra."

"But you sing, Eddie," said his mother. "You have a beautiful voice."

"But I haven't been asked to sing," said Eddie. "Anna Patricia's bratty little cousin, L.C., is going to sing the Christmas songs with the orchestra. Imagine being a boy called L.C. Everybody thinks L.C. has a wonderful voice, but he won't sing unless he's given a box of chocolate-covered marshmallows."

"Poor Eddie," said his brother Rudy. "He can't sing in the Christmas show and no marshmallows for him."

One evening later in the week his father came home and handed Eddie a box. "Here, Eddie," he said, "this isn't a box of marshmallows, but it may get you into the orchestra. You show this to Mr. Saunders, who trains the orchestra."

"Oh, Dad," said Eddie, as he opened the box, "what is it?"

"They're bells," said his father. "I had planned to give them to you for Christmas, but with your sense of rhythm I think Mr. Saunders will let you join the orchestra."

Eddie lifted the lid of the box. "Oh, look," he exclaimed. "The name of this instrument is inside the lid. It has a funny name. G-L-O-C-K-E-N-S-P-I-E-L."

"That's right," said his father. "It's the German name for bells."

Eddie sat down and began playing a tune on the bells. "Hey, I can play it," he exclaimed. "I'm a musician."

Eddie rushed to the telephone because he felt he had to tell somebody about his musical instrument. He dialed Anna Patricia's number, and when she answered, he said, "Hey, Annie Pat, what do you think? I'm going to be in the orchestra!"

"You're not going to be the vocalist," said Anna Patricia. "My cousin is going to sing."

"Oh, no, I'm going to play an instrument," said Eddie.

"An instrument!" Anna Patricia exclaimed. "What are you going to play?"

"A glockenspiel," said Eddie.

"A what?" said Anna Patricia.

"A glockenspiel," said Eddie, a little louder.

"I can't understand you," said Anna Patricia.

"You should speak better English, Eddie."

"I'm speaking German," said Eddie. "I just learned it."

"Well, what can you say?" said Anna Patricia.

"Glockenspiel," said Eddie. "It's the instrument I'm going to play in the orchestra."

"Well, I never heard of it," said Anna Patricia. "And I don't believe there is such a thing."

"Yes, there is," replied Eddie. "You just listen and I'll play it for you." Eddie placed the telephone right beside his instrument. He picked up the hammers and struck the bells. He played a little tune. Then he picked up the telephone and said, "Did you hear it?"

"Yes," said Anna Patricia. "It just sounded like bells."

"That's what it is—a glockenspiel," said Eddie.

Eddie could hardly wait for Monday morning to come. The weekend had never seemed so long. On Monday he would go to the orchestra for rehearsal. When his teacher said, "The boys and girls of the orchestra may go to rehearsal," he would get up and go along with Anna Patricia and Sidney and the others who were in the Christmas television program.

At school things did not work out just as Eddie had expected. At half past nine Mr. Saunders sent for him. Eddie carried his case down the hall to Mr. Saunders's office.

When Eddie opened the door Mr. Saunders saw a very different boy from the one he had said good-bye to on Friday afternoon. This was a very happy Eddie indeed.

"Hello, Eddie," said Mr. Saunders. "Let me see your bells."

Eddie placed the case on a table, opened the clasps, and lifted the lid.

Mr. Saunders placed a sheet of music on the stand and said, "Now let's see what you can do with this."

Eddie began to play, but he found that playing from notes was not as easy as picking tunes out by ear. He began to look worried.

"It's all right, Eddie," said Mr. Saunders. "You will have to learn how to play it."

"But I played it all right over the weekend," said Eddie.

"That wasn't playing, Eddie," said Mr. Saunders. "That was picking."

"Do you think I'll be able to play it in time for the Christmas concert?" asked Eddie.

"If you work at it, I'm sure you will be," said Mr. Saunders.

Eddie stayed with Mr. Saunders for a half hour working on his bells. He didn't go to orchestra rehearsals. This was a disappointment, but Mr. Saunders said it wouldn't be long before Eddie could be part of the orchestra. Eddie worked hard and the following Monday, when he went to Mr. Saunders for a lesson, he did quite well.

It was not long before Eddie went to practice with the orchestra. This was a very important day to Eddie. His place was right behind Anna Patricia.

It took some time for the violins to tune up, but at last Mr. Saunders raised his stick. "Eddie," he said, "you know where to come in, don't you?"

"Yes, sir," said Eddie.

"I know where he comes in," said Anna Patricia. "I've been helping him."

"Eddie is the one who has to know where to come in," said Mr. Saunders. "Now, all ready?"

Everyone was ready, and the orchestra began to play one of the Christmas songs. Eddie watched his music carefully and when it was time for him to play the bells, he came in right on the beat. As he struck the bells and the sound blended with the rest of the instruments, he felt a tingling that went up his back and his neck, right up into his hair.

Eddie thought the music was beautiful. He hadn't ever realized that music was so beautiful, and he was doing something to make it beautiful.

Now it was time for the bells to be silent for a minute. Eddie held his hammers and looked up at the ceiling. He was listening to the music and thinking about Christmas. When it was time for Eddie's bells to come in again, Mr. Saunders nodded to Eddie, but Eddie was busy looking at the ceiling and thinking how beautiful the music was.

Anna Patricia saw Mr. Saunders nod and she knew that it was time for Eddie's bells. She took her clarinet out of her mouth and said, "Hey, Spielglocken! Wake up!"

This stopped the music. Everyone, including Mr. Saunders, laughed. Eddie's face turned red.

"Eddie," said Mr. Saunders, "you will have to keep awake."

"Oh, I'm sorry," said Eddie.

That was the morning that Eddie Wilson became Eddie Spielglocken.

Eddie kept his mind on his work after that, and

he did very well, but all the boys and girls in the orchestra now called him Eddie Spielglocken. Eddie didn't care what they called him. He was happy. He was in the orchestra at last and he was going to play in the Christmas television concert.

* 6 *
The Christmas Concert

The orchestra had been rehearsing for weeks for the television concert. Mr. Saunders was pleased with the children's work. They practiced at home, and this meant that the rehearsals went well. Anna Patricia's cousin L.C. was to sing three Christmas songs. He came to each orchestra rehearsal and sang the songs. It took a great many rehearsals before Mr. Saunders was satisfied with the orchestra accompaniment. By the time he was pleased, every child in the orchestra knew the words of the songs by heart.

At home, Eddie's twin brothers whistled the

tunes over and over, and Eddie sang them every time he took a bath.

Mr. Saunders had made his plans very carefully. The children were to go to the television station in the school bus. Each child was to take care of his own instrument and to be sure to have it with him when he reached the studio. The concert was to go on the air at nine-thirty in the morning, which meant that the bus would have to leave the school promptly at eight-thirty. Mr. Saunders told the children that everyone must be at the school by eight o'clock. This was a half-hour earlier than anyone had ever gotten to school before.

The thing that had not been planned was the weather. It had begun to snow the day before. It went right on snowing all night and turned into the first blizzard of the winter.

It was still dark outside when Eddie's mother snapped on the light and said, "It's still snowing. Daddy and Mr. Stewart and Rudy and the twins are all shoveling the snow out of the driveway. Mr. Stewart has to get the car out, because he has to take Sidney and her cello to school. He says he will take you and the twins also."

"Am I glad!" said Eddie, looking out of the window. "Boy, is it deep! Poor Mr. Saunders."

---------------------- ✳ ----------------------

When Eddie's father and his brothers came in from clearing the driveway, they were cold and hungry. The boys ate piles of buckwheat cakes with maple syrup and drank big cups of steaming hot cocoa.

At half-past seven Mr. Stewart blew his horn, and Eddie and the twins gathered up their things. Eddie had his glockenspiel and each of his brothers had a saxophone.

"I feel sorry for the fellow who has to carry the bass drum this morning," said Mr. Wilson.

"That's Buster Bronson," said Eddie. "He plays the drum."

"Poor Buster!" said Mr. Wilson, as the boys departed.

Sidney's father had to drive very slowly because it was snowing so hard it was difficult to see ahead. When they reached the school, the big yellow school bus was parked by the curb at the back of the school. Snow was piled on the roof of the bus and on the hood and fenders. It stuck to the windows and windshield.

Mr. Stewart carried Sidney's cello up the steps and into the school. "Do be careful, Sidney," he said. "When you go out to the bus, don't slip with the cello."

"I'll be careful," said Sidney.

As the children in the orchestra gathered in the hall, Mr. Saunders told them exactly what to do. "Eddie," he said, "be careful with your bells. Sidney, watch out for your cello."

"Sure, Mr. Saunders," said Eddie. "Sidney, you better be careful you don't take a bellyflop on your cello."

"We'll go out the back door," said Mr. Saunders. "It will be easier to go down the back path than down the front steps."

Eddie ran to the back door and looked out. "Two men are shoveling the path," he said, "but there's an awful lot of snow out there."

"Remember that you'll be going downhill to the street," said Mr. Saunders. "Take it slowly."

"Where's L.C.?" said Sidney.

"He isn't here. His mother is taking him right to the studio," said Mr. Saunders.

"What about the marshmallows?" said Eddie. "He won't sing without that box of marshmallows."

Mr. Saunders laughed. "Maybe he will give you one, Eddie," he said.

"Not a chance!" said Eddie.

Now all the children had arrived, and the time had come to leave for the television station. The men who had been clearing the path had finished. They had moved around to the front of the school.

"Come along," said Mr. Saunders. "Drum goes first, and take it easy."

The path was narrow and already icy. They went single file, Buster first, carrying the drum, and Eddie behind him. They had not taken more than four steps when Buster's feet slipped from under him. The drum flew out of his hands and started rolling down the icy path toward the street.

"Hey!" cried Eddie, just as he fell over Buster.

"Oh! Oh!" cried the boys and girls who were standing in the open doorway.

"There goes the drum!" cried Sidney. "There goes the drum!"

While Eddie and Buster were picking themselves up, the drum was rolling along, gathering up snow as it went. Half-way down the hill it ran plumb into a first-grade boy. It knocked him into the deep snow and went on its way. It rolled through the open gate and out into the street. By this time it was well on the way to becoming a great big snowball.

The members of the orchestra watched in horror. They expected a car to smash the drum as soon as it reached the street. But it rolled on. Eddie and Buster ran after it. So did Mr. Saunders and the bus driver. The drum rolled across the street into a big snowdrift. It was so heavy with snow that it almost plowed right through the snowdrift. It was exactly as though it had gone through a door.

The men pulled it out and scraped away the snow. Then Mr. Saunders carried it into one of the buses.

Eddie found the drumsticks in the street. "Good thing I found these," he said to Buster.

Mr. Saunders was relieved when he finally had all of the children in the bus with their instruments. As they started off he said, "Now if L.C. shows up, we're all right."

"He'll show up," said Eddie. "He'll show up for the chocolate-covered marshmallows."

When the orchestra reached the television studio, the bus driver and Mr. Saunders helped the children out of the bus and into the building. The orchestra was taken to a room to wait until it was time to go into the studio. The room was right next

to the studio, and the wall between was a glass window. The children could see into the studio, and there was a lot to see. Very few of them had ever been inside a television studio. L.C. was the only one who had ever been on a program, and he wasn't there yet.

Eddie had his nose right against the window. He didn't want to miss anything. He could see a beautiful lady standing at the end of a great big room. From a very high ceiling hung huge lamps, which made the brightest light Eddie had ever seen. The beautiful lady was standing behind a shiny white kitchen table. In back of her there was a stove and a kitchen sink. She was mixing something in a bowl, but Eddie noticed that she wasn't looking at the bowl. Instead, she was looking straight ahead, talking and smiling, just as though somebody was there. While she talked and smiled at nobody, two men moved around her with great big cameras. Another man on a little truck raised and lowered a long pole with a microphone on the end. Eddie couldn't hear a thing, but he could see everything.

"Mr. Saunders," he said, "are we going to give our orchestra concert in that kitchen?"

"It won't be a kitchen when we go in," said Mr. Saunders. "All the kitchen will be moved away."

Suddenly, from down the hall, a child's voice cried out, "Where are my marshmallows?"

"Here comes L.C.," said Eddie.

Then there was a scream. "I won't do it! I won't do it! I won't sing!"

Uh-oh, thought Eddie. Something has happened to the marshmallows.

L.C.'s mother appeared in the door with her son. "Oh, Mr. Saunders," she said, "a dreadful thing has happened. My husband drove off with the box of marshmallows by mistake."

L.C. was yelling now. "I won't sing! I won't sing without the marshmallows'!"

"L.C.," said his mother. "You are going to sing. I want no more crying over marshmallows."

If they called me L.C., Eddie thought to himself, I would make them buy me a whole candy store.

L.C. went right on yelling. "Aren't you ashamed, L.C.?" asked his mother.

L.C. was not ashamed. He just yelled louder than ever.

"Now, L.C.," said his mother, "I want this nonsense stopped. The marshmallows are safe in

69

Daddy's car. Daddy isn't going to eat the marshmallows. You can have them as soon as you get home."

Mr. Saunders was watching the clock, and Eddie was watching the beautiful lady in the kitchen. Now she was taking a cake out of the oven. It looked good. Eddie hoped they would all get a piece.

"L.C.," said Mr. Saunders, "you'll have to stop crying. We go on in five minutes."

L.C. began to quiet down and finally he stopped crying. But now he had the hiccups. His mother went to get a glass of water. When she returned, she handed the glass to L.C. and said, "Take ten sips."

L.C. took ten sips and hiccupped again.

"He should stick his fingers in his ears while he drinks the water," said Rosalie.

L.C. stuck his fingers in his ears and his mother held the glass for him. Most of the water went down the front of his sports jacket and soaked his bow tie. He hiccupped again.

"Put a key down his back," said Buster. "That will stop it for sure."

L.C.'s mother opened her purse and took out a key. She dropped it inside L.C.'s shirt collar. L.C.

hiccupped again and said, "It didn't go inside."

"I know how to stop it," said Frank. Then he whispered to L.C.'s mother, "I'll scare him. That will fix it." He went to the door and stepped out into the hall. He pointed with his finger down the hall. "Oh!" he cried out. "There's a big rat out here!"

Every girl in the orchestra screamed, but L.C. just hiccupped.

"Are you crazy, Frank?" said his twin brother.

"No," replied Frank. "I was just trying to scare the hiccups out of L.C. But it didn't work."

Now Mr. Saunders received his signal to take the orchestra into the studio. At the Wilsons's house, Eddie's mother had turned on the television set. She was pleased to have three of her boys playing in the orchestra and excited because they were going to be on television.

When it came time for the songs, Mr. Saunders made an announcement. "We have had to change our vocalist," he said. "Eddie Wilson, who plays the bells, will now sing three songs."

When Eddie stepped out in front of the orchestra, he remembered the lady who had made the cake in the television kitchen. He looked right out at nobody. But the whole time he was singing, he made believe that he was looking right at his mother's face.

And he was, for his mother was looking right at her little boy and feeling very proud of Eddie, who was singing his Christmas songs.

When he finished, he just said to everybody, "A merry Christmas to all!"

* 7 *
New Toys from Old

The children in Eddie's third-grade class had decided to make this Christmas a real sharing time. The class had decided to bring toys that could be repaired as gifts to the children in the nearby hospital. Cars had to be repainted, wheels had to be put back on trucks, and new dresses made for the dolls.

Eddie and his friends set to work to make the toys as good as new. Many fathers and mothers helped.

The children not only brought their own toys but they also collected some from neighbors and brought them to school. The toys were piled in one corner of the room and the pile grew larger every day.

One morning Eddie was sitting beside the pile of toys fastening a wheel back on a truck when Anna Patricia came in with a doll. As she placed the doll beside the other toys she said to Eddie, "This is a nice doll but she looks washed out. She needs to have her cheeks made rosier and her eyes made a pretty shade of blue. Eddie, you fix her up, and some little girl will be very happy when she gets this doll."

Eddie looked up at Anna Patricia and said, "Don't bother me now, Annie Pat. I'm trying to put this wheel on this truck. Put the doll down and I'll take care of it when I've finished with this truck."

Anna Patricia put the doll down and said to Eddie, "Well, just remember, Eddie, her cheeks have to be made pink and her eyes blue. Don't get mixed up."

Eddie groaned, "How could I get mixed up? Don't I know that cheeks are pink and eyes are blue? I'd be crazy to paint her cheeks blue and her eyes pink."

The children laughed. "Well," said Anna Patricia, "you do crazy things sometimes, Eddie."

"Just don't bother me," said Eddie. "I'm busy."

Eddie's friend Boodles heard everything that Anna Patricia had said, and he thought it would be fun to play a trick on Eddie. Boodles loved to play tricks.

After awhile, when Mrs. Aprili had told the children that they could read or paint, Boodles went over and picked up the doll. He carried it to his desk where his box of watercolors lay open. He mixed some blue paint with some water and quickly brushed it onto the doll's cheeks. Then he mixed a little red paint with some water and dropped it into both of the eyes. The paint dried quickly and in a few minutes Boodles placed the doll beside the other toys.

Eddie, still busy with the wheel of the truck, had paid no attention to Boodles.

Later in the morning Anna Patricia picked up the doll. A scream came from Anna Patricia. "Oh, Eddie Wilson," she cried. "How could you be so mean?" Anna Patricia carried the doll to her teacher and said, "Just look what Eddie Wilson did to this doll. He did just what I told him not to do. He's made her cheeks blue and her eyes pink. No little girl will want a doll that looks like this. Eddie has ruined this doll."

"What do you mean?" Eddie cried out. "I never touched the doll."

"Well, someone did," said Mrs. Aprili, "because this doll now has blue cheeks and pink eyes."

Some of the children thought this was very funny, but Eddie didn't laugh. Eddie was mad. "I'll bet Boodles did that," he said. "It's just his kind of a trick."

"Boodles," said Mrs. Aprili, "did you do this?"

Boodles hung his head and said, "Yes, I did it. I was just having some fun."

"Well," said his teacher, "now you can have some fun getting this paint off."

"It's just watercolor," said Boodles. "I haven't ruined the old doll, and Eddie can paint her green if he wants to, and see if I care!"

Boodles dipped a cloth into some clear water and in a few moments he had washed the doll's face and her eyes. He handed the doll to Anna Patricia and said, "Now she really is washed out."

Anna Patricia put the doll back with the other toys, and before Eddie went home that day, he gave Anna Patricia's doll a beauty treatment and turned her into a perfect Christmas gift for some little girl.

One morning a toy horse joined the pile of toys. It was a pure white horse and Eddie thought it was beautiful. But Boodles thought he could make it more beautiful, and before the end of the day, a zebra had joined the toys. Boodles had painted black stripes on the horse. When Eddie saw it he said, "Where did this zebra come from?"

"It just got born," said Boodles. "Now don't tell me to wipe it off 'cause it's oil paint, and if I wiped it that would just make a messy gray horse! And besides, I like zebras!"

"Okay," said Eddie, "maybe some kid will like a zebra for Christmas, but I'll bet Santa Claus never received a letter from a kid asking for a zebra for Christmas."

When the zebra was dry, Boodles placed it with the other toys.

The pile of toys grew larger every day. The classroom began to look like a toy shop.

One morning Eddie and Boodles were kneeling beside a pile of toys. They were sorting them out when Mr. Sam came into the room with a large carton. "I'm going to put all of these toys into this box," he said, "and I'll keep them in the basement until the day comes to take them over to the hospital."

"We'll help you pack," said Eddie.

"Sure," said Boodles, "we'll hand them to you."

"Okay," said Mr. Sam.

When the box was filled Eddie said to Mr. Sam, "You will be careful won't you, Mr. Sam? You won't let anything happen to this big box of toys, will you?"

"Don't you worry about them," said Mr. Sam. "I'll remember that this carton has a great big letter *D* printed in blue on the side. It won't get mixed up with anything else."

Every Thursday morning a truck appeared outside of the school to pick up the week's rubbish. The Thursday before Christmas, when Eddie arrived at school, he saw the truck parked by the curb. The driver and his helper were packing cartons into the truck.

Just then Boodles joined Eddie and he suddenly pointed to a carton that one of the men was putting into the truck. Boodles grabbed Eddie's shoulder and cried out, "Oh, there goes the box of toys into the truck."

"You're right," said Eddie. "It's the box with the big blue *D* on it."

The driver was already in his seat and his helper had jumped into the back of the truck.

"Quick, Bood, we've got to stop 'em," Eddie shouted. Eddie began to cry out, "Wait, wait," but the truck went on. The boys raced up the sidewalk trying to catch up with the truck, yelling, "Wait, wait, wait!"

Finally the boys saw the truck stop by the curb. The boys knew that the driver must have seen them in his mirror because the truck was waiting and the driver's helper was standing beside the truck.

The boys, all out of breath, ran to the man and Eddie said, "You've got a carton full of the toys for the children in the hospital."

"Toys?" exclaimed the man. "What makes you think we've got a carton filled with toys?"

Eddie pointed to the carton and said, "It's that one with the big blue *D* on it."

"That's right," said Boodles. "Mr. Sam packed all of the toys into that carton."

"Well," said the man, "we certainly don't want to take the children's toys away. I'll take that carton off and we'll look inside."

"Oh," said Eddie, "we all worked very hard fixing those toys to go to the children in the hospital."

"Sure did," said Boodles. "It would be terrible if they were taken to the dump."

"Sure would be," said the man, as he placed the carton on the ground. "Now, let's look inside and see if it's full of toys."

Eddie and Boodles watched as the carton was opened and they both looked inside. "See any toys in there?" the man asked.

"Oh, Bood," said Eddie, "we've made a mistake."

"It's just full of paper," said Boodles.

Eddie looked up at the man and said, "I'm sorry, but you see we helped Mr. Sam put the toys into a carton just like this one with a big blue *D* on it, and when we saw you put it into the truck we thought it was our toys for the hospital."

The man grinned and said, "Well, boys, it's better to be safe than sorry."

The man's helper put the carton back into the truck and climbed in the back. As the truck started off, the men called back to the boys, "Merry Christmas, kids."

And Eddie and Boodles called back, "Merry Christmas to you."

* 8 *
The Christmas Program

Eddie had been selected to be Little Boy Blue in the Christmas program his class was giving at the hospital. When he told his mother she said, "Oh, that's good, Eddie. You were Little Boy Blue in the first grade, and I still have the costume."

"But, Mom," said Eddie, "I'm much bigger than I was in the first grade."

His mother looked at him and said, "You're a little taller but I think the costume will fit you."

When the great day arrived Mrs. Wilson watched Eddie as he put on his Little Boy Blue costume. "Mom," said Eddie, "I'm going to bust right out of these pants."

"Don't be silly," said his mother. "You'll be all right. Just don't do any violent exercise."

"Okay," said Eddie. "But they're awfully tight."

When Eddie reached school he did not rush into his classroom as he usually did. Instead, he walked carefully, and Boodles said to him, "You walkin' on eggs this morning?"

"Mind your own business," said Eddie, and he sat down on his chair carefully.

When Anna Patricia arrived she was wearing a beautiful white dress because she was to be Snow White in the afternoon program. Everyone admired Anna Patricia's dress.

At lunch there was tomato soup, and Anna Patricia carried her bowl very carefully and set it down on a table. Then she sat down and spread her dress around her. In a few minutes Eddie came over to join her. "Be careful of that soup, Eddie," said Anna Patricia. But Anna Patricia had spoken too late. As Eddie put his bowl of soup on the table, some of it splashed out onto Anna Patricia's white dress.

"Oh, Eddie," cried Anna Patricia. "Look what you did!"

"I'm sorry," said Eddie. "I'll dip my napkin into my glass of water and I'll get the spot out."

But Eddie didn't get the spot out. He just made it worse.

"Oh, no," said Anna Patricia, "now I am a mess."

When the children returned to their classroom Anna Patricia showed her dress to Mrs. Aprili and said, "Just look what Eddie Wilson did to my dress. I look like a Campbell kid instead of Snow White."

Her teacher looked at the dress and said, "Don't worry about it, Anna Patricia, there's a Laundromat in the next block. Eddie can run up there and be back with your dress in a few minutes."

"I'm sorry I can't take her dress to the Laundromat," said Eddie, "but I can't run because my pants are too tight."

"Well, Boodles," said Mrs. Aprili, "you take Anna Patricia's dress to the Laundromat."

"Okay," said Boodles, "but it wasn't my soup that splashed on her. I'll take it because I'm so good-natured! 'Good-natured Boodles'—that's who I am!"

Anna Patricia took off her dress and put on her

coat and Boodles went off to the Laundromat. Soon he was back and Anna Patricia put on her clean white dress.

Now Mr. Sam came into the room dressed as Santa Claus. "I'm all ready," he said, "except for my beard. I put it down some place in here."

Eddie held up a paper bag and said, "Is this it, Santa Claus? I nearly sat on it."

"That's it," said Mr. Sam. "It wouldn't be right to have you sitting on Santa Claus's beard."

This made all of the children laugh.

At two o'clock Mrs. Aprili led the children out to the school bus. Santa Claus brought up the rear with the big carton of toys.

When the bus stopped at the hospital a nurse led the whole group into a large room where there were many children gathered. Some were in beds, some in wheelchairs, and many sitting on folding chairs. When they saw Santa Claus they all clapped their hands.

When the third-grade children were seated, Mrs. Aprili spoke up. "Boys and girls," she said, "we are delighted to be here this afternoon. Santa Claus has come to give you your presents."

The children, with wide eyes, watched Santa

85

Claus open the big carton. Then he began to hand out the presents. Soon there were voices all over the room.

"Oh, look at my beautiful doll."

"Oh, I have a red car."

"This is a great truck."

Then above the sound of all other voices, was heard, "Oh, oh, oh, I have a zebra. It's just what I wanted. I love zebras. Look, everybody. Look at my zebra!" A boy in a bed held up the zebra, and Boodles was glad he had put the black stripes on the white horse and made a little boy so very happy.

After all the toys had been distributed Mrs. Aprili said, "Now we have a Christmas program for you. You will see characters from nursery rhymes and from stories you all know, but we have made some changes that we think you will like. First of all, here is Little Boy Blue."

Eddie stood up, but instead of blowing a horn, he beat a drum that was hanging around his neck, and said, "That'll get 'em out of the meadow and out of the corn."

As Eddie sat down there was the sound of a rip and Eddie knew that what he had feared had happened. His pants had busted! Eddie felt his face turn red. He was sure his underpants would show through the rip. What should he do? Just sit still, he decided. But what if he had to stand up and sing "The Star Spangled Banner?" But it was Christmas, not the Fourth of July, so they wouldn't be singing "The Star Spangled Banner." His coat was over the back of his chair. He decided to put it on because it would cover the rip. He knew he had to be quick. Eddie wiggled around trying to reach his coat but he had to get up after all. As he did a great roar of laughter came from the children. Eddie was sure they had seen the rip in his pants, but they were laughing at Santa Claus whose beard had suddenly fallen off. Eddie, with a great sigh of relief, put on his coat, just as Santa Claus, with a great sigh of relief, put his beard back where it belonged.

"Now," said Mrs. Aprili, "we have Jack Be Nimble."

Boodles stood up, holding a candy cane instead of a candlestick. He put the candy cane down on the floor and jumped over it. Everyone in the room clapped their hands.

"Now," said Mrs. Aprili, "we have Snow White and the Seven Dwarfs." Anna Patricia stood up and seven children gathered around her. They

stooped down trying to make believe that they were dwarfs. Then they began to sing, but instead of singing the song of the dwarfs, they sang "Rudolph, the Red-Nosed Reindeer," and because all of the children knew the song, everyone in the room sang "Rudolph, the Red-Nosed Reindeer."

Mrs. Aprili spoke again. "Now we have Goldilocks and the Three Bears."

Jennie, wearing a large blonde wig, stood up and said, "I'm Goldilocks." Then a very plump boy said, "I'm Papa Bear." And a girl said, "I'm Mama Bear." Then Jennie's little sister from the kindergarten said, "I'm a, I'm a Suzie!"

"Oh, no, not this morning," said Goldilocks. "Now tell them who you are."

The little girl began again. "I'm a, I'm a Suzie Bear."

"You are not a Suzie Bear," said Goldilocks. "Now tell them who you are."

Whereupon every child in the room called out, "Baby Bear!"

"That's right," said the little girl. "I'm Baby Bear."

Then one of the third graders, wearing a red cape, stood up and said, "I'm Red Riding Hood and I'm looking for my grandmother."

A girl rose up and said, "I'm your grandmother."

"But you don't look like my grandmother," said Red Riding Hood.

"Oh, that's because I've just eaten the wolf," said Grandmother.

"Oh," said Red Riding Hood, "in my story the wolf ate you!"

"Well, in my story," said Grandmother, "I ate the wolf. Right tasty!"

"Now," said Mrs. Aprili, "you're going to hear from Alice in Wonderland."

A girl and a boy stood up and the girl said, "I'm Alice in Wonderland and this is the Mad Hatter, only he forgot his hat."

The boy made a bow and said, "Sorry about that. I'm supposed to be mad and invite you to a tea party, but I'm not mad and there isn't any tea!"

"No," said Alice in Wonderland, "but there is ice cream and you're all invited to our party. Santa Claus, bring out the ice cream."

All of the children in the room clapped and clapped and clapped, and soon they were all eating ice cream.

When the day was over everyone felt very

happy, and the third graders went home knowing that the Christmas vacation had started off with a bang!

When Eddie reached home he said to his mother, "I busted out of my pants all right. I busted out good!"

* 9 *
The Mystery of the Christmas Cookies

One day, the week before Christmas, Eddie said to his mother, "Mom, what can I give to Mrs. Aprili for Christmas?"

"How would you like to give her some Christmas cookies?" his mother asked.

"Sure," said Eddie. "Cookies would be a nice present. What kind?"

"I'll make chocolate-chip cookies," his mother replied. "Everybody likes chocolate chip."

The following afternoon Anna Patricia came in to play a game with Eddie. They were in the midst of the game when Eddie's mother said, "Eddie, you will have to go to the store and buy some chocolate chips so I can make the cookies for Mrs. Aprili."

"Okay," said Eddie. "Come along, Annie Pat. Let's go get the chocolate chips."

"Sure," said Anna Patricia.

The children ran off to the store and Eddie bought a bag of chocolate chips. "I just love chocolate chips," said Eddie.

"Me, too," said Anna Patricia.

"My mom won't mind if we eat a couple," said Eddie, as he held out the bag.

"You sure?" said Anna Patricia.

"Oh, sure," Eddie replied. "She always gives me some when she's making chocolate-chip cookies."

Anna Patricia ate a few and Eddie ate a few. Then they both ate a few more and a few more. They ate chocolate chips all the way home.

When they reached the house Eddie put the bag on the kitchen table. His mother was beating up the batter. In a few moments she reached over for the bag of chips. "Why, Eddie Wilson," she cried, "there aren't enough chocolate chips in this bag to put in this chocolate-chip cookie batter! Where are they?" she asked.

Then before Eddie could answer, she said,

"Never mind answering me. I know where they are. There is chocolate all around your mouth. You've eaten them."

"I'm sorry, Mom," said Eddie. "I didn't know we were eating so many. We just ate one at a time."

"Well, now I can't make chocolate-chip cookies," said his mother. "And the batter is all ready so I'll just have to make raisin cookies."

"Raisin cookies are good," said Eddie. "I think Mrs. Aprili will like raisin cookies. Maybe even better than chocolate chip."

"Well, that's what she's going to get," said his mother, as she watched Eddie write his name on a little card and put it into the box for the cookies.

It was already Friday. The class had taken the toys to the hospital and given the Christmas program. It had been an exciting day, and Eddie was still excited. He was so excited he left the box of cookies on the kitchen table when he went off to school.

When he came home his mother said, "You forgot the box of cookies for Mrs. Aprili."

"I know," said Eddie, "and now school is closed for the Christmas holidays. But Mrs. Aprili only lives two blocks away and I can take them over this afternoon. I'll go right now."

"All right," said his mother. "When you pass the bake shop, go in and buy a loaf of cheese bread and some cinnamon buns."

"Okay," said Eddie, as he picked up the box of cookies. "See you later, Mom."

When Eddie reached the bakery he put his box of cookies on the counter and asked the clerk behind the counter for a loaf of cheese bread and six cinnamon buns. The clerk put the bread into a bag and the cinnamon buns into a box. Eddie picked up the bag and the box and left the shop. But his box of cookies was still sitting on the counter.

In a few minutes a little girl came into the shop. She asked for a loaf of cinnamon bread and six doughnuts. The clerk behind the counter put the bread into a bag and the doughnuts into another bag. Just then the telephone rang and she picked up the receiver. She talked a long time while the little girl waited. When the telephone call was over the clerk said, "I'm sorry. I'll put everything into a sack for you." She put the bread and the doughnuts into a sack and picked up Eddie's box of cookies and put it in too.

The little girl didn't notice the cardboard box.

She got into a waiting car, saying, "Sorry to keep you waiting Mommy, but I couldn't help it. There was a telephone call."

Just as the car drove away Eddie burst into the shop. "I left a box of cookies on the counter," he said. "Did you find it?"

"A box of cookies?" said the clerk. "Did you buy them here?"

"No," said Eddie. "My mom made them for my teacher. Didn't you find them?"

"No," said the clerk. "I guess you left them at home."

"Well, maybe," said Eddie, "but I thought I had it with me."

"You're mistaken," said the clerk. "I think you'll find it when you get home."

When the little girl and her mother reached home her mother emptied the sack. When she saw the cardboard box she lifted the lid and said, "I didn't tell you to buy cookies."

"I didn't," said the little girl. "I just bought the bread and the doughnuts."

"Well, what about these cookies?" said her mother. "Lucy, you must have bought the cookies."

"Well, I didn't ask for any cookies," said Lucy.

"Maybe the clerk gave them to us for Christmas. She said, 'Merry Christmas.' "

Lucy's mother picked up the telephone. "I'll call the bakery," she said.

When the clerk answered, Lucy's mother said, "I'm afraid Lucy didn't pay for the cookies."

"Cookies?" said the girl. "What kind of cookies?"

"They seem to be raisin cookies," said Lucy's mother.

"We don't make raisin cookies," said the clerk. Then she added, "I'm sorry, madam, but I'm very busy putting up orders. It's Christmas, you know, and I don't know anything about raisin cookies." The clerk hung up the telephone.

Again Eddie burst through the kitchen door. "Mom," he said, "I didn't leave the box of cookies for Mrs. Aprili here, did I?"

"No," said his mother. "You took them with you. You were going to take them to her home. You probably left them at the bakery when you stopped to get bread and cinnamon buns."

"But I went back to the bakery," said Eddie, "and the clerk said she didn't see any box. Oh, rats, what should I do?"

"I'll tell you what to do," said his mother. "You

go back to the bakery and buy two pounds of their cookies and take them to Mrs. Aprili. Here's some money."

Eddie went off to the bakery and bought the cookies. As the clerk was putting them into a box, Eddie said, "Do you have a Christmas card I can put in with the cookies?"

"It's a little one," said the clerk, "but here it is. You can write your name on it."

Eddie wrote his name on the card and put it in with the cookies. As he went out the door he called back to the clerk, "Have a merry Christmas."

And she said, "Same to you."

When Eddie reached his teacher's home she was out so he left the box with the young woman who answered the door.

At Lucy's house everyone ate raisin cookies over the weekend. Lucy's father liked the cookies, her mother liked the cookies, and Lucy liked the cookies. They ate them with tea, they ate them with ice cream, they ate them by themselves.

By Monday morning there were very few cookies left in the box. At lunchtime Lucy's mother took another cookie and, to her great surprise, she uncovered Eddie's Christmas card. She picked it up and read it to Lucy. "Oh, Lucy," she said, "this box of cookies was for Mrs. Aprili from Eddie Wilson."

"Well, Mrs. Aprili teaches the third grade in our school," said Lucy.

"Well, now," said her mother, "a large box of cookies has just arrived from your grandmother. I'll just fill up the box, put the card back in, and drop it off wherever Mrs. Aprili lives. I'll look her up in the telephone book."

Late in the afternoon Lucy's mother left the box of cookies at Mrs. Aprili's house.

Mrs. Aprili was surprised to receive two boxes of cookies from Eddie Wilson. She liked the ones from the bakery very much indeed, but the coconut ones that had come from Lucy's grandmother she thought were the best Christmas cookies she had ever eaten. They were so good that she decided to telephone Eddie Wilson's mother and ask her for the recipe.

When Mrs. Wilson answered the telephone Mrs. Aprili said, "Oh, Mrs. Wilson, those coconut cookies that I found in the box from Eddie are the most wonderful cookies I have ever eaten. I should like to have the recipe."

"Coconut cookies!" exclaimed Mrs. Wilson. "I don't know what you mean."

"Oh, yes," said Mrs. Aprili, "the ones covered with white icing and candied cherries."

"Oh, no," Mrs. Wilson exclaimed, "I just made raisin cookies for you."

"Well, there was just one raisin cookie in the box," said Eddie's teacher.

When Mrs. Wilson hung up the telephone, she said, "Eddie, that was quite a mix-up with those cookies, but Mrs. Aprili seems pleased with her Christmas present."

After that Eddie always called raisin cookies mystery cookies, because for Eddie the mystery of the cookies had never been solved.